at the helm of twilight

Anita Endrezze

Broken Moon Press ◼ Seattle

Some of these poems have previously appeared in these or earlier versions. Publication information appears at the end of this book.

Printed in the United States of America.

ISBN 0-913089-26-5
Library of Congress Catalog Card Number: 92-70015

Cover image, "Path of the Red Deer II," by Anita Endrezze. Used by permission of the artist. Author photo copyright © 1991 by Dave Danielson. Used by permission of the photographer.

Thanks to the Weyerhaeuser Company Foundation and to Bumbershoot® for choosing this book for their 1992 publication award.

Broken Moon Press
Post Office Box 24585
Seattle, Washington 98124-0585 USA

at the helm of twilight

For my children
Aaron Joseph Sunhawk
and
Maja Sierra Rose

Contents

I have three names

Desert Rose.   Stormy.   Grace.

I have three shadows.
I have a white owl
that drinks all my words
straight.
I have a red deer
that lets me cry on her back.
I have a black snake
that shows me my old skins.
I have three coffins
waiting for me
to make the wrong move.

Sometimes three names
are not enough
to sing about...

at the helm of twilight

I was born

I was born
husk of jelly-
fish
afterbirth
like a blood orange

I was born
in a storm
the rain white as milk
small priestess of sand-
waves   sea rust   salt grass

I was born
above Los Coyotes Boulevard
where because it's California
there are no coyotes
and not far from the river
which had no water,
only cement

I was born
with one leg twisted
toward the womb
Was I dreaming
of running away
from life?

No. I was born
with the ancient river
in my bones
visible as the blessing
in my eyes

Because I was born
in storm's eye
in the vortex of spirit
I could see the yerba buena
in the milk
waves of poppies
yellowing in the dry wind
and lunar horses
trembling in the bamboo

in short   I was born
in a body
that renews the soul

I was born
little palm heart
little
shadow
of a greater one

The Girl Who Loved the Sky

Outside the second grade room,
the jacaranda tree blossomed
into purple lanterns, the papery petals
drifted, darkening the windows.
Inside, the room smelled like glue.
The desks were made of yellowed wood,
the tops littered with eraser rubbings,
rulers, and big fat pencils.
Colored chalk meant special days.
The walls were covered with precise
bright tulips and charts with shiny stars
by certain names. There, I learned
how to make butter by shaking a jar
until the pale cream clotted
into one sweet mass. There, I learned
that numbers were fractious beasts
with dens like dim zeros. And there,
I met a blind girl who thought the sky
tasted like cold metal when it rained
and whose eyes were always covered
with the bruised petals of her lids.

She loved the formless sky, defined
only by sounds, or the cool umbrellas
of clouds. On hot, still days
we listened to the sky falling
like chalk dust. We heard the noon
whistle of the pig-mash factory,
smelled the sourness of home-bound men.

I had no father; she had no eyes;
we were best friends. The other girls
drew shaky hopscotch squares
on the dusty asphalt, talked about
pajama parties, weekend cookouts,
and parents who bought sleek-finned cars.
Alone, we sat in the canvas swings,
our shoes digging into the sand, then pushing,
until we flew high over their heads,
our hands streaked with red rust
from the chains that kept us safe.

I was born blind, she said, an act of nature.
Sure, I thought, like birds born
without wings, trees without roots.
I didn't understand. The day she moved
I saw the world clearly: the sky
backed away from me like a departing father.
I sat under the jacaranda, catching
the petals in my palm, enclosing them
until my fist was another lantern
hiding a small and bitter flame.

Sanctuary

When I was a little girl I believed
I could move clouds by breathing
my straw-thin breath upward,
and whispering "sanctuary."
When I was older, I was Given Responsibilities,
but the sheets would mold in the dryer, forgotten
as the lunch dishes I put in the oven.
Sister gloated: You'd even burn corn flakes.
Mother complained: You're always off
in your own little world.
I made my eyes as blank as butter
while she furiously scoured the pots.

In my world, their voices were distant
as Saturn's rings. Mistakes were written
in sand during a fierce wind.
My world was small as a ship in a bottle,
a terrarium Eden, or the Lord's Prayer
etched on the inside of a needle's eye.
My world was as big as the seasound
in a shell, as the pollen that drifts
across the seas, as the single cell algae
conquering ditches with a phalanx
of green shields. This is my secret:
my world regretted nothing, not
burnt toast (which was Night Squared)
nor the lies of boys with eager hands.
Nothing mattered but the mantra
of a cricket, or the chanting
of the maple's leaves in their high mass.

The Banana Tree

It grew in an uproar,
the leaves unfurling
from a central stalk
like a whirlwind.

I knew:
there were large black spiders
living in the center...
there was rain that smelled
like red jungle soil...
there were the yellow eyes
of an Amazon Indian
silently watching.

I winked, deciding even then
to love the unknown.

These bananas were not edible.
They were for decoration only.
They weren't like the supermarket ones,
plump, curved.
I liked them better
for their blackened fingers,
their unpalatable tongues.

My mother decreed the tree uncivilized,
ungainly. It lacked the proper proportion
in our lives.
She chopped it down,
but rebellious daughter that it was,

it grew back
overnight
bearing illicit fruit.

She hacked it down again.
It rose up
on the third day
and I whispered,
hand at my throat,
"Lord Yellow Eyes, is it you?"

There is a resurrection promise
no mother can tolerate:
the forgiveness of her daughter's sins.

This time she hired two men
with their manly shovels
and hard-sworn axes.
"Eve's tree," they laughed
and set to, with a furious pace
not even life
could keep up with.

They carried away
every last leaf and bone of it,
every root and spare heart of it,
until nothing was left
but a hole big enough
for a whole tribe
of pagans
to be baptized in.

"Better to plant pansies there,"
my mother directed.
Better to see small obedient faces
looking up at you,
than the wild mocking eyes
of wayward daughters.

Beautiful Mothers (1988–1772)

Montana salmon in the pearled foam of rivers
Jean Ann Endrezze

roses bloom in the kiln of the coastal fog
Ann Elizabeth Kambrič

halos of heliotrope: flowering in your name
Empimenia Flores

slender fingers on a 12-string guitar
Charlotta Ramos

red lace on your dark hair, pistols on your hips
Estefana Garcia

stout as a white potato, polka dancing over the copper mines
Elizabeth Yaeger

rose, attar of red stars, Slovenian woman
Joanna Ostronič

he should've given you rubies instead of rocky fields
Giuliana Slanzi

a white-washed house, passionate red flowers
Sussie Ameser

the gray fields, his hand on your bright hair
Marija Petrič

narrow streets, mud or cobbled, the sky with too much dignity
Barbara Streljar

coral-skirted dancer
Orsola Tavonati

behind: the Alps; at your knees: children
Anna Mottes

slender girl threshing autumn
Ana Mravineč

did you dream of violets, violins, and milky skin?
Margareta Verdin

the Cardinal lit 10,000 candles for your catlike smile
Felicita

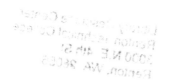

The Mapmaker's Daughter

the geography of love is terra infirma

it is a paper boat
navigated by mates
with stars in their eyes

cartographers of the fiery unknown

it is the woman's sure hand
at the helm of twilight, the salt
compass of her desire

the map of longing is at the edge
of two distant bodies

it is the rain that launches thirst
it is the palm leaf floating on waters
far from shore

the secret passage into the interior
is in my intemperate estuary

the sweet and languorous flowering
is in the caliber of your hands

the circular motion of our journeying
is the radius of sky and sea, deep
territories we name
after ourselves

The Magician's Daughter

The air is thick with rabbits.
I am a little bored
with that trick. And always
so white! Out of *thin* air?
Even the rabbit knows better,
having left behind thousands
of herself in a limbo of fur
and pale eyes. It is we
who are invisible.
She is shocked
at our hands pulling
her through.

And the scores of knotted scarves
that the magician believes in!
I long to untie each one.
I want to see him pull his bones
out of his fist. I want
an illusion of sacrifice.

Speaking of which, enters the girl.
She climbs in the box, waves.
I watch her wiggle her toes.
When he cuts her
in half, she still smiles.
Like the rest of us,
she thinks she is whole.

The Dieter's Daughter

Mom's got this taco guy's poem
taped to the fridge, some ode to celery,
which she is always eating.
The celery I mean, not the poem
which talks about green angels
and fragile corsets. I don't get it,
but Mom says by the time she reads it
she forgets she's hungry. One stalk
for breakfast, along with half a grapefruit,
or a glass of aloe vera juice,
you know that stuff that comes from cactus.
And one stalk for lunch
with some protein drink
that tastes like dried placenta,
did you know that they put cow placenta
in make-up, face cream, stuff like that?
Yuck. Well, Mom says it's never too early
to wish you looked different,
which means I got to eat that crap too.
Mom says: your body is a temple,
not the place all good Twinkies go to.
Mom says: that boys remember
girls that're slender.
Mom says that underneath all this fat
there's a whole new me,
one I'd really like if only I gave myself
the chance. Mom says: you are
what you eat, which is why she eats celery,

because she wants to be thin,
not green or stringy, of course,
am I talking too fast?
but thin as paper,
like the hearts we cut out
and send to ourselves,
don't tell anyone,
like the hearts of gold
melons we eat   down
to the bitter rind.

The Jester's Daughter

The farmer's son
is eyeing me;
his little brown heifer
is jealous.

The banker's son
is counting on me;
his interest
is mounting.

The poacher's son
thinks I'm fair game.
The priest's son
believes in the Word Made Flesh.

I humor them

because it's the miller's daughter
with her leaven breasts,
her hips the breadth of my breath,
whose floury hands
touch my heart.

The Juggler's Daughter

I can keep my eye
on more than one body
at a time;
the trick is in
not becoming attached
to what will drop you.

Swords, plates, balls, rings:
they relieve the monotony
of juggling
affairs.

It's up in the air,
love is;
if it's not where you think
it should be,
be quick! what comes next
may stab you in the back.

We all love a good trick
we can't figure out.

When we're not in love,
what we miss
is the balancing
between faith
and what the eye knows
is really there.

The Undertaker's Daughter

Who could love
these cold hands?

Who could love this cooling
heart?
Who could love this body smelling
of drains, knives?

Who could kiss
these shoulders,
which will inherit
bones?

Who could love
this dead–white face
the mouth set in a lifelike smile
on this face
I see
in my mirror?

The Idiot's Daughter

mocking, jeering
ya make wide eyes
when I walk by

dareya! dareya!
call me crazy

I don't care
if he wears a crown of bread
and butterflies
he's all I got

so if my old man has sprung
a sprocket
so what
if when he hangs up his jacket
he first forgets to off it?

it signifies nothing
this dim
wit of a peach pit
this
life

The Medicine Woman's Daughter

A charm to keep you part of the whole

May the white bark be nine times your mother
May my burnished cheeks be twice sun-daughters
May the apple that divides seeds into simple stars
      be the multiple of your life
May my breasts be the marigolds in your night garden
May the dark broom that is your shadow be a memorial
      to your father
May you live between my thighs and in my heart
May lapwings rise at your feet from every crossroad
May I be in between your two hands the way sky is
      the center of beech dreams
May our love be the mystery of wind and the soul's
      duration
May your life be as charmed, as strong, as the single
      white rose blooming in snowy circles

The Alchemist's Wife

Late you work, clinking glass vials,
waving your hands over mud and cow spit,
dreaming of gold or stars solidifying
by morn. You wander in the fields
collecting the first dew after a full moon
or the yarrow that wilts from the tears
of a lame girl. The village women give you
their hair clippings to bind a rope to heaven.
Even the priest saves altar dust for you,
although your skills, so far,
have saved only Thomas' old sow.
While I, unpraised, am the true alchemist:
From the fevers of our children,
I light the hearth fires.
From their shivering nakedness,
I spin transparent robes.
From their swollen bellies,
I fashion empty bowls
fit for the Emperor of Bones.
And when their breath is gone,
I place pebbles on their eyes
so they will forever see their father's love.

■ ■ ■

Sometimes being married

is like killing time—
and then the ticking clock
stops.

"I haven't worn this shirt for a year,"
he says resentfully
"because it has no buttons."

I look critically at the needle,
closing one eye
in order to recognize
our anatomical predestinations.

I see the thread
on the spool
wound too tight
and liable to break
at the least tension.

I put the needle down,
the thread. So.
My lap is empty.
Husband: there's nothing left
worth mending.

Waking

My tongue is not a thorn.
My heart is not carbon.

For the first time I see
my body in its own light.
It's beautiful.
My breasts are small planets
containing seas with tidal desires,
or else: two bells of earth,
two nipples trembling
like soft leaves.

The insides of my knees are acknowledged:
virginal aunts who kept their faces
turned away, unremarkable
to men. And therefore, unsung.
No more!
I'll know all of my body
the way the seed knows the plum.

And I will love myself.
The dark rose folds of my vagina,
like a bottle of flesh
filled, fulfilled, in itself.
My fingers know its wine
which is salty like a peach
rolled in your hands.

And the autumn colors of my thighs,
the balconies of my shoulders,
the hidden nape, ripe
with tender skin,
the hair unknotted,
and dark.

The hair between my legs is soft
and straight.
It is nothing to be ashamed of.
It roots in the female sea.

My knees are the faces
of stone sphinxes
worn down
by time.

My ankles are filled with silences.
They are better than wheels.
They are verses of Uprightness
and Responsibility.

My toes are peanuts, earthed,
unearthed. They enter the darkness
of the sole
with faith
and forgetfulness.
Little daughters: you keep me humble.

Searching for the One in My Dreams

There is no Compass of Dreams. North is not the home of lost birds. Red is not the color of neighing horses. You do not ride a gray wolf into my circle.

Nothing is where or what it's expected to be: not your name on my tongue dissolving into sweet syllables. Not whiskey-talk around Coyote's fire. Not your strong body I boast to know.

Like any dreamer, I am lost. You could step out of my dreams in T-shirt and jeans, singing about owls and I wouldn't know you. Your face is not used to being loved. It is only an image of what my hands want to cup.

White birds across the dark leaves of fall: this is you. Your name is a red branch. Your eyes have been the western twilight. Your mouth knows my passionate direction. Though you be the only rain on a high plateau, I will find you.

Offers

1

a man sent me caribou antlers
he said he'd marry me if I'd have children
otherwise, he'd find another woman
and call her by my name

2

a man gave me whiskey
we sat in an old bottle-green car
the swans in the sea were like flowers
floating in the fjord

we pretended to be married
we pretended to be strong enough to believe
that the birds held the sky back

3

a man gave me a rake
its tines as thin as my fingers
he gave me a garden full of weeds
find the rose, he said,
and we'll marry
when he smiled his teeth were like thorns

4

a man gave me colored stones
to weight down my neck
so that my breasts would droop into his hands

I'd marry you if you were bigger,
he said, or your hair shone yellow
in the dark

He said: I'd marry you ten times
if you were someone else

5

a man gave me pages in his book
he gave me promises we both understood
to mean less than a finger's trace
in the air

my lips were red and full
his wife hung her wet laundry
and looked at him with a beggar's eyes

6

I wonder if marriage is between two people
the way sky is between two birds?

Twelve Love Poems

He laughs. When he does, I mysteriously think
of alabaster lamps, small candles within,
lighting up the dark with their opalescence.

When he laughs, I dream about fistfuls of sky
and moonwheels that turn tides.
I hear the galloping of stone horses,

little fetishes that the earth strings
around her throat.

2

Who is wiser?
the lover or the beloved?
the match or the flame?

Perhaps it has nothing to do
with wisdom.
I've turned my back on knowing
hands before.
Will this man touch me
in a different way?

His hands are strong and gentle,
like two halves of the same lion-eyed rose.

3

I danced in the snow,
my mouth open,
burning
in the cold air.

You smiled at me
and suddenly,
the snow melted
on my cheeks.

4

Yesterday
I saw an old lover
drinking out of a brown paper bag.
"It's a shame how life distorts
such fine wine!"
he laughed.

For a moment, I held him
tenderly, remembering
how we once unashamedly
drank
in
our nakedness.

5

All night the drunken swaying
of my hips
has left you dreamless.

Now the swollen sun
rises among the peach trees.

Don't leave. It's night yet.
Close your eyes and see
how my hips still ripen
in your hands.

6

The wind is a man
I know by touch.

I wear a green dress
he lifts.

7

All night long
I dreamt of you.
I rubbed my cheeks
upon your thighs
and dreamily kissed them.
Am I too bold?
You can't protest now
when your eyes
undress me so.

8

In the next room
you sleep with your wife.
I listen to your breathing.
Outside the gentle wind
blows out
all the candles in the trees:
the leaves fall like burnt wicks
onto the water.

Which of us are you dreaming about now?

9

Beloved, haven't you noticed
how thin I've become?
Look how my rings fall off
gold and silver
and the way the moon shines
through my hips . . .

You don't neglect me but
in the absence of water
I'd drink my own blood.
In your absence
I am consumed
by my own hungers.

Look: on my dark shoulders
white birds of prey.

10

Once I watched the stars burn circles
in the night, wishing
all the while for a friend,
a lover who would be flint
to my tender.

Now. . .

11

My house is full of candles.
I burn constantly.

I hold them in my palms.
I carry them in grass cups.

My body is full of stars
and the confusion of flames.

Since I have lain with you,
all others are darkness.

Since I have loved you,
I've come out of my dark animal shape.

Since we have parted,
I'm not part of the flame
and hurt.

Dearest,
don't let the nearness of stars
remind you of broken candles.

12
I've given up violets
dried in heavy books;
instead I gather the dark pinwheels
of stars and press them
on my breasts.
I'm an independent woman.

Love?
I open my veins.

These Are Roses You've Never Given Me

These are roses you've never given me.

They grow upon the wild bush,
their petals bitten by wind.
They sleep with owls,
these roses.

If you could, you'd place them
in my dark curly hair.
You'd find my mouth
among the pink petals
and, wildly, I'd open
to your tongue,
your palm,
your shaking touch.

You would not be naked,
covered by wind
and the shadows of clouds.

I would not be naked,
covered by you
and the roses pale as ash.

I am your mistress, your lover,
the one with volcanic eyes.
I carry roses in my name:
nocturnal roses the texture of thunder,
dream roses made of water,

sea roses curling in salt,
tropical roses made of wood,
wheat roses rising like bread
in the heat.
Roses made of teeth
and threads of rain.
Roses: gifts of love,
labial and violet.

I Give You

I give you secret horses
wreathed in jasmine.
I give you yellow wine
distilled from aged stars.
I give you my tapering thighs
which are two slender candles
joining in flame.

I give you the power to touch fire.
I give you the dreamy tunnels
midnight makes in our sleep.
I give you my wet hands.

I give you the aquamarine eyes
of rain.
I give you the lost map
to my bed.
I give you my onyx eyes
that see even in the dark
shadows of your thighs.
I give you the noble crown of love.

I give you the buttons of silence
inside a snail's shell.
I give you the hurricane
of my orgasm.
I give you the evidence of ocean
in my womb.

I give you the green corridors
grass divides from the wind.
This we have forever:
this fragrant entrance,
this opening to each other.
I give you this. I give you this.

In the Kitchen

1

There are some eggs white as flour.
I put these white eggs in a blue bowl:
they are the bells of winter.

Some wives believe that eggs should be hollow—
they prick the shell with a pin
and suck out the yolk and white.
What they blow back in is all
their emptiness:
the eggs sound thin
as the shell of a moon rolling
against the iron cold rim of night.

2

The fork has a masculine urge   jab
and thrust, forcing the tongue
to remember its sense of duty.
A spoon is a woman's tool:
lap, sip; and open like a petal.
The knife has its place
in my heart. It can be angle
of night-clipped moon
or the sharp edge of a kestrel's cry.
It's neuter in its purest mission:
cut, slice; the Law of Frugal Movement.

3

This plate is like a grandmother
with a warm, round face
and flour on her cheeks.
She is giving me sweet rolls
and cinnamon tea in an egg white cup.
She says: you will marry
the first man you love
and pick apples together
in an old orchard.
I want to tell her:
the man is already in the orchard
and his wife is making applesauce.
I'm only waiting for her to fall asleep,
tired, with her red hands pulling the blanket
up to her chin—and my own hands
pulling her man down into the headiness
of the sweet-fallen apples,
our lust both ripe and raw
and as temporal.

When I Am Mute

For when I am mute
the rain water growls
in a black bowl
and I am a red leaf
floating
or a drop of blood
from a full womb.

For when I am mute
the candle flames
like an ivory orchid
like a man's finger
turning over
inside of me.

For when I am mute
and the voices are owls
screaming in the cellar,
their eyes circles of rage
not wisdom
and their talons
are my fingers
at the moment sleep
leaves me.

For when I am mute
let the dogs howl in their wet fur
and the roses bloom underground
and the red and green apples

twist under the knife,
falling on the white cloth
like sweet parts of myself.

Let the mice nest in my throat
for when I am mute
I am full of helpless words
and my eyes are like angels
after God has torn off their wings.

For when I am mute
it is because your words mean too much to me
and not the sea which moves so beautifully
in my walk and not my own two hands
which convince my skin of silk.
For when I am mute
the glass is always one sip short,
as if you were there before me,
and doors will not open
because I have no magic sound of my own.

Yes, the muteness is its own scream:
the sea roaring inside a glass ball,
roses blooming in honeycombs,
my heart beating with fists of silk,
my eyes closed shut, flameless,
against my need for you.

Storm

1

The trees are dancers with birds on their shoulders.
The earth's a fast drum and wind's my elemental skin.
The rain breaks
into green leaves.

2

Or: the night was still as red pollen
and the birds were only small knots of darkness
the wind was weighted down by the genealogy of grass
the trees carved totems in the clouds
and the rain was still
in the catacombs of the sea

3

And: waking, you reach out for the long dark clouds of my hair
gathering this summery body, this storm
closer
your mouth aching for the center,
the fire in the rain

■ ■ ■

The light that passes through stones

is the same light that reddens the apples

the light that lingers to green
the wheat is the same that whitens
the insides of chestnuts

the light that is the coronation
of my hair is the same light
that gloves your hands

the mouth that is the wolf of the North Wind
is the same mouth that blackens
the blossom

the mouth that is the voice
of floods is the same that consents
to the joining of clay and sun

the mouth that is the companion
to sunflowers of honey is the same
that kisses you

the white horses that break
their necks on the sea-cliffs
are the same that blow softly
among your apple blossoms

the eyes that see stemfuls of light
are the same that see the matriarchs
dancing in mountains

the eyes that see warships in skeletons
are the same that see stars in egg shells

the eyes that see you walking in the grass
when there's nothing but the wind
are the same eyes that see
distance sealing a great door

Skål!

First, there's the barbaric moon
that looses her white mares
adorned with bells of opal:
this aquavit makes me fanciful.
My throat burns.
You place a fingertip between my breasts
and my eyes widen.

It's that kind of night.

Before you knew me,
I had fallen into a throat of stones,
into the facelessness of sand.
Unsure, I changed my hair style.
I practiced walking away
from myself.

Here have another.
Look at the moon's Scandinavian hair
and the white roses tucked insolently
behind her ear. She laughs
and you remind me that in Danish
to get married means the same as being poisoned:
gift.
We look at each other steadily,
hopeful and brave.
So, we'll get married this summer
we decide

after the moon has tossed back
a couple more drinks
and whistled her mares home
and we are left,
wrapping the reins of darkness
around our wrists.

The Wedding Feast

Hørby Faergevej, September 9, 1989

There are plates of rye bread and herring
and small glasses of aquavit
and amber-colored beer strong enough
to put ten Vikings under the table
but I keep tilting my cup up
not wanting to let my tribe down.
There are pâtés of pheasant and lean Danish pork
and delicate slices of cucumber
pickled as the eleventh Viking
who tries to dance with me,
his belly big as a boat.
There is more beer
and transparent slivers of smoked salmon
that taste as soft as butter
and thin slices of dark bread,
and there is more beer
and my tribe
is losing ground.
There is no time
for sleep or fresh air,
although the harbor wind is brisk.
There is more beer and I see red
and white faces, swaying like flags
and at last I understand your national colors.
There are songs as long as Beowulf,
in Danish, which I can follow pretty well
until there is more beer.

There are platters of ham and crusty white bread.
There are pale spears of asparagus
and four kinds of cheeses.
There is smoked eel and baked salmon with fennel.
There are people here we don't even know.

We are married
and assured of a tax break.
We are married,
with our elbows propping us up on the table
and full of beer
and two kinds of cake
and pickled onions and beef with grated horseradish on top
and with each round of skål!
the fishermen pop open another beer.
My son, who carries a bottle opener,
has been adopted by everyone.
We are married and tired
while your parents dance on,
their hot Viking blood
out-dancing this Indian.
They give us a black horseshoe for good luck
and cut off your tie and throw rice
down my blouse and then there's more beer
because the rice was rather dry

and after coffee and cake, we are escorted
to our room in the kro* by the sea,
by Vikings with fiery sparklers and beer

*country inn

and this Indian
says no to the video camera focusing in on our bed,
where after the door is shut
and we're alone and quiet,
I admit my defeat and desire
to sleep
and you, descendant of Vikings who could row
with one arm all the way to Sicily and back,
(using the other arm to hoist horns of beer),
are already snoring.

In the Horizontal Sky

(twelve views)

1

we see the Queen of Heaven
weeping over the thousand candles
or golden, smiling, extending her hands to heal
so that the crippled will rise
and fall from greater heights

and when water withers into sleep
it offers us fingers of drought
we can pray then
for the rivers to empty the sky

we can imagine the horizontal sky
is god lying down on the job

we can see the whirlwinds become dancers with holes
where their eyes should be

the sky itself has eyes as vacant as milk
it takes all our beseeching looks and makes stars
that collapse in on themselves

2

I was born with nothing to hold on to

I crossed into the threshold of bones,
into my mother's arms,
black hair wet on my head,
the scarlet moon hissing in the sea

3

plants have eyes to follow the sun
you say my eyes are beautiful
and leave my bed dazed and dry-mouthed

later we watch the night sky, the stars buzzing
like a wasp's nest

4

around my neck, tiny agate birds sleep
against the circular nesting of my bones

5

in the trees' great silences
are our mothers' faces

6

among scholars, there is always the question:
who was where first?

for example, 7,000 years ago
in the Arctic, there lived a mysterious red-painted people

in the dark sea, thickened with salt and cold,
their white-flashing oars smelled like the breath of trees

we know their houses were rectangular
we know the sea was their foundation
the cod, the whales, the black curve of wave

we have carbon-dated their tools
we have measured their skulls
we have studied their bodies folded into the solitude of earth

we have seen shadows migrate from the lean wave of bone
to the whale-eye moon

7

when I'm in love I take an inventory
of the stars
yes, love, I am sustained by the horizontal

it doesn't matter who comes first!
in your blue eyes is the marrow of sea minerals

8

the black locust trees drip with nectar in spring
and the bees float like cinnamon-colored petals
over the picnicker's white loaves

there is a hill nearby that shimmers in green light
where children tumble down
out of the sky

9

I've put sky-blue sheets on our bed
when we sleep, your hands will caress the dark moons
of my body

10

there are reports in the cities
of a wondrous people whose bodies are outlined with white clay
and whose eyes are as beautiful as Nefertiti's

we don't know where they came from
or why
we don't know why the sky perpetuates itself
in their hour-glass bodies

11

Lately, I've been asking myself:
am I candle not finished with burning?

and is your body, beloved, a bird made of snow?

12

Or is one question enough
to loosen the sky from your hair?

Sunflower Woman

(a poem to be read in vertical or horizontal columns)

holy sunthroat
a constant caress
floral prophetess
we both are

corn sister
my love is the root
of golden harps
waters of topaz

undeciphered
the ancient language
with obsidian eyes

we are hieroglyphs
meaning
woman skywise

our lovers know
the slender body
the bones of lightning
breasts of petals

our hair unbound
like thunder clouds
thighs of sweet
honey centers

sunflower hair: burnt scarf
dark radiance
my hips rotate
under his fingers

mine's a leafy branch
or the aura of stars
circular butterflies
mythical female birds

I am three ways
in his bed
the gold of sea water
the moon's crown
the tender mouth

a sunflower
wind's hour
seminal tides
nocturnal swelling
of desire

Sunflower sienna
madonnas
dueñas
wanton shoulders

clay face
sky pillars
medicine circles
chaparral chaparones

Your lover is in the air
                in fire
in the wind
O! wrists of saffron!

O! tongues of
Yomumuli
gold plumed snake

the flaming water in
stems with voices
singing rain
the yearning throat

from the suntree
at night in his hands
the luminous wings
awaken

sister tiger-eye!
I desire
the noon's erectness
oceanic womb
waves of breath

we both are
wild dancers
crazy eyes
moon–drunks

Sunflower Woman *(continued)*

I'm afraid
sister: give me
rivers of silver
sierra madres
anything to keep me
loved

I'm afraid to trust
we wear out   from men
bracelets of compromise
earrings of betrayal
necklaces of cheapness

Sunflower woman
know my soul
the way the blind
seeing yellow in
the sunlight
crying out

wise sister
stela greening
black diamond seeds
sister wise

it becomes a chant
language
songs

he won't love me!
a pyramid of yellow
dreams
unfolding
in his heart
Beloved!

sister
we've eaten shit
said yes
meant no
meant yes

give me hope
let trust
be
the dawn
rising
whole

spider sepal
earthbloom
tendrils
he will not leave

a miracle
of gold bells
secreted in granite

always
fibrous light
in turquoise cups
into gold masks
strong unbeaten
free

I know
we gave shit   got
ground under heels
flipped the finger
begged for it but

let his hands
be two ways
the adornment
of my nakedness
in the blackest night
undivided

solar funnel
borders of pollen
line your bee eyes
he will not leave

in the everyday
we turn into
stone fetishes

Sunflower Woman *(continued)*

ah
wet roses
circlets of sky
flowering

he mouths my nipples
tawny birds
I grow beautiful
in his harrowing

but
sister my self
my skin is single
a summer
of long glances

will he stay?
a woman's question
the goddess blossoms
on the soft tree
deep kisses

stay
I hold his seed
in my hands
my womb
sinuous curves

come
in my mouth
the hot rain
my palms blessing
my woman's body

at noon
we see the same
we do not want to be
alone without love
silent

the sun passes on
the knowledge of life
alone
without faith
solely

dark bronze buds
fruiting
ankles of air
the seeding o o o

kachina
thunder-flower
prayer sticks
the hard tree
under the holy moon

come
the twilight horses
consecrating
the horizon's
eternal motion

through
the flower's eye
blood sister
our faces
a halo of light

Song Maker

There is a drunk on Main Avenue, slumped
in front of the Union Gospel Mission.
He is dreaming of pintos the color of wine
and ice, and drums that speak the names
of wind. His hair hides his face,
but I think I know him.

Didn't he make songs people still sing
in their sleep?
Didn't coyote beg him for new songs
to give to the moon?
Didn't he dance all night once and laugh
when the women suddenly turned
shy at dawn?
Didn't he make a song just for me,
one blessed by its being sung only once?

If he would lift his face
I could see his eyes, see
if he's singing now
a soul-dissolving song.
But he's all hunched over
and everyone walks around him.
He must still have strong magic
to be so invisible.

I remember him saying:
Even grass has a song,
'though only wind hears it.

Ways to See

1

a waterfall is one way river sheds its skin
a boiling pot is the steam's cradle song
the black night is what's left of weather-eaten stars
the flowers are the way the dead see

2

I hardly know myself anymore
my hands are two place mats at an empty table

I follow strangers, looking for your face
I wander, untouchable desire, invisible

3

with my desolate lips I drink
from the dry pot that scorches the minerals

I know the skin that receives nothing but the dusty caresses of stars
I see the night dispersing into the dark branches of water

4

in my hair, a dried flower that seeks my moist oils
in my mirror, the face of a woman
    who sits down to drink from an empty bottle
    to stare at the river's dry shadow
    to see the minerals in her eyes give depth to her grave face
    to find the night entering darkly through the mouth
and to know, oh, the sad ways the heart boils dry

Last Harvest

man woman horse tree
the woman's mane is pure wheat
released in late autumn light

you are living for the sky to empty
itself into your heart
you are waiting for horns of dust

to drift at your feet
from the shadowy herds
in the shy widow's meadow

you believe the harvest is your body
and the woman is gathering your ripeness
with her small sleepy hands

but she is only dreaming
of her own body slipping
under the warm surface

she is sighing a name
and it's not yours

Perceptions of Three Birches

1

Between them, three indigo daggers
of thunder, or three twisting suns,
and the gardens of the moon,
with its three white ponds
surrounded by translucent periwinkles.
And the moon's three breasts,
or else the unspoken
knowing in the dark iris
of your eyes.

2

These are your favorite trees:
always in a triangle
of tangled air and centers
that could charm us
into a knot of thighs and arms.

3

But you are less distracted,
not seeing the twiglike eyes
and the flat leafy tongues
constricted by our circling.
Not hearing the columns of animals
that imagine the sounds of their teeth clicking
to be the way trees speak.

4

Three: always equidistant from each other,
like three white moths
around a flame. Fascinated.
A man and two women facing each other,
around a table set with milk and white rags...
Or else, a bed with only two pillows.

5

Imagine the bark unrolled
and written on
in a language with only three sounds.
Or painted with white horses
carrying naked women freed from slavery.
And three green stars
tumbling out of the parchment
into the hands of children.

6

What *you* see are just three crooked birches.
Birdless. Sky balanced
by solid trunks,
not the shadows leaning
like mourning women,
their white eyes
shining in the dusk.

7

Just once, I wish you'd forget
that stars belong in the sky
and find the three birds of love
in my hair and undo the time
on your wrist
so that the only passage you know
is the sun floating into the dark
and then, the passage into me,
which is like palms of water,
like a mouth of flames,
like a circle of tree-women holding hands,
like trees of lightning
within us.

Calendars

the days are circles of bread, paper-words, the light in the egg
the nights are grass-moons, volcanic glass,
    the dark wine of the body
the calendar of water is lightning-flint, the dew that scars
    the iris, the bitter salt of blood

my wrist is time's turning on bone, the sinew of grace

the sky is an enormous shadow
over us all   the eternal questions
whose shadow?   whose time?

the calendar of stone is gold and sand, the blind eye
    of fossils, dust layered on cold water

the calendar of crosses depends on the sin of the wood
the calendar of sin depends on the carpenter's measure

the tongue seconds the loins; the heart beats
in the plum's falling, the pulse in the slender neck

there is time enough for everything, they say
time enough for orange to become red,
the November-colored hair to turn white,
the ice to keep time with the cracking of stars

the calendar of dawn is in the good-byes,
the lovers' last looks,
the milky dream of thighs

the healing transforms the open wound,
heart or skin, into moments of pure clarity

we know our mortal limits
thousands of leaves nest in the earth
we lay down our flesh for joy or death

the calendar of bones passes, unnoticed and obvious

November

A litany of rain. Leaves strain
like tethered birds to thin twigs.
The raked piles I roughly stacked
have scattered. Winds rush
from my bones, whistles of seasonal loss.

What I feel in November
is no accident. My face is a hollow lantern;
I carry it through my darkness.
Is it a beacon, or a negative light,
like the sky around migrating birds?
The geese angle their perfect flight;
I have their need. My body consists
of the same angles. Its imperfection
stuns me.

What We Believe

We believe in a land where sweating horses
kick up the dust, forming clay ponies
that sigh with red and yellow breaths.

We believe in a grass-weaver,
whose fingers make gentle blankets,
trusting in green, yellow, and brown.

We believe the horses will wear our blankets,
will drift forever past our campfires,
listening to us telling stories of long ago.

We believe that long ago we were horses
and grass, that our stories are our children's
dreams. We are waiting for the sound of hoof-beats

to rise from our throats and for the tall grasses
to stamp and snort in the wind. What we believe
will always be—and always be true.

Reviewing Past Lives While Leaf-Burning

The air is a smoke-tree, the wind
is the song of branches burning
into a brief sleep. I breathe the atoms
of yellow leaf and crumbled sun
until I am back scraping lichen
from the nest of rocks, my old eyes milky
as quartz. I know the names of seven winds
and seven colors and the herbs that heal
and I see the flocks of crystal birds
mending the sky where it cracks each morn,
but I am old. Tribeless. My skin breaks
its oath to me, leaving me unfulfilled.
I see palms of smoke in the air
and badgers tunneling under my song
until I become a young boy
riding the red mare in my father's herd,
following the fog off the coast.
Close by, the sacred island is a black hip
in the sea. There the priestesses
like boys with dark eyes.
I can only remember the smoke that whispered
like a woman and her fluttering tongue
that she called fire and my father's face
far away crying in the mare's mane
until I became a woman, beautiful in my veils,
beckoning my dark hand to the fisherman
who never returns, my lungs turn to smoke,
my bones to luminous shells, my voice as nowhere

as the wind. Then I am blonde, kneeling
in the fields only men till, scratching out
the grave of my girl-child whose father
would not take her to our hearth
and my breasts are smothering in ash,
the milk dripping into the earth where fog
rises with its sucking mouths and I keen,
believing only in the horned hands of death.
Yet, I am born again to smell the bitter
cordite of guns as the bullets burn the air
into little flags of resistance.
It is the last bullet that narrows
my name to earth and sky
takes my faith on its lips to praise.
Nearby, smoke hovers over the barracks,
singing *sarahabrahamrebecca.*
Until, at last, I am here: burning
leaves and my life as a woman
is full of everyday happiness:
the grasses are seeding the air
with green blessings, my husband
fills my room with red roses,
and my son is my only jewel,
until I am loved and loved and loved
and still, it's not enough.

After the Last Plague

The village was still,
dreaming of stones.
I buried two babes
under ash and oak.
My husband is a hearth
for dead songs.
An old woman came
to the door;
it was me.
I carried ash
under my tongue.
I cut my hair
into black sheaves.

I took my harp
into the fields
and sang to a sky
that rained salt.
I broke the christian
man on his cross.
I broke my tears
into rocks the shape
of crows.

Now my breasts
are like nests
in winter;
my hips ladders
into the earth.

Claiming Lives

1

The woman who jumped off Monroe St. Bridge
into the drumming river, left a note
written on an old newspaper:

"My head's full of rippling birds,
my heart is a firmament of water.
My eyes are basalt angels.
Help the small fish I swallow."

They waited days for her to surface,
but her body fell through sun-stringed waters,
down, down, into the deeper calms
she'd always dreamed of.

2

Cold, cold: water ribs protecting hearts
of fin and heron. Water vaulting over
submerged Chevies, drivers still gazing
at veils of windows, their hands stretched forth
as if they were still beating
against the blue-green wings.

Under the bridge, the river's as fervent
as a hallelujah revival. Later, the river
divides itself into rambling duck grass
and mud-plopped pasture. It bursts
into the memories of red-winged blackbirds,
mists over ancient fishing grounds, floods
its waters with rare Northern lights.

Deep in the water's veins, its minerals
are human. The water is painted red
by cougar tongues. There is a song
we can hear when it rains on the river:
it is the Song of Consummation.

3

A man is lost under the yellow canoe.
He has a strange memory of sun paddling
deep into his skin. Now he is learning
the language of clear open waters:
grasshoppers clicking inside fish bellies,
the constant belittling of sand.

Soon he will go to the Water Village
whose totem is Salmon and Beaver.
He will see all the water-spirits,
their wispy bodies curling inside
watery holes, skin smoothed down
to rhythms of snow and dam turbines.
Their eyes are as beautiful as the scales
of rainbows in deep pools, their hair
like fishermen's nets of fluid reins.

He will hear them sing about moon spawning
and cattails probing the mud
for drowned children.
He will see the woman whose whole life
was a hollow reed. She will embrace him,
claiming the debt we all owe
to those who die as they were born:
in broken waters.

Canto Llano

All the sisters of mercy
have joined their flat hands,
piercing their palms with roses;
blood ribbons a garland
las flores del psalmos,
las monjas han llorado pérdón.

Las diosas del fuego, me devoré:
como las caras de los santos.

They are a white-hooded coven
of falcons crying;
the slow spread of lilies
growing deep under graves.
Too many hail marys
rot bones as they save.

They are circling
burning round
thick in chants at Yucatán.

Creo ver a Dios
en la locura de sus ojos;
las lunas rojas
las lunas llenas
misa rezada
de trébol blanca.

Their ankles taste bitter
burning round
eyes of dark waters.

Mis hermanas de Sangre Diosas
canto a sus hijas brujas.

All the sisters of mercy
are pregnant with moons.
They circle me,
fingers smoking like candles;
they roll their own stones.
I am on my knees.

In the House of Animals

Each room is a journey away
from the falcon's tether,
the occasional understanding
of the sky's dismantling.

What dimensions we take
depends on the shadows
we leave behind

My wolf husband trotted silently
beside me, nudging my shoulder

He brought me gifts
of limp-necked birds
(they felt the sky coming down
into the grass and their wings
migrated into the earth)

They were only guests in a field of rain
we came through the same door
we opened the same window into the mouth
of life

As a bear, who fears the dark coffin
of earth? The birch trembles,
its red hearts suspended in the wind.

Each room is the distance
between breath and sleep

What we wake into is flying before us

Snow is an animal with old eyes
our voices are fragments
of that remote falling

Only the wild geese remember
the stairs in the sky
and the room at the top
where our souls are given eyes

Fox-Woman Goes Man-Hunting

Not far from the waterlight flickering on scattered aspen, I take on the illusion of womanskin. How my eyes grieve at the mammalian moon: its perfume is caught in my shrugged-off fur. The ancient way to-become-a-woman is a secret of russet and ghostgrass. And one foxword spoken into the dew.

I know the ins and outs of this. Have stolen clothes off the line before, gone past chickens with only a twitch of my hips. So now I grab a shirt and some pants. Some old boots on the porch.

It's nightdark, larkspur-blue, and the stars blinking like frightened mice. They say First Fox was a Vixen. She saw her reflection in the pond water and called it forth. She mated with this liquid-eyed Waterfox on a bed of clover. When morning came, he had gone back into the dew.

I hitch a ride into town. Guy who drives a white pickup says I'm a sassy-looker. Tries to paw my breasts, but my teeth are closer to the throat and blood-seasoned. He kicks me out, but that's OK. Got some hunting of my own to do.

First Fox was desolate. She ran back to the pond but the fog was seeping out of birchbark and the water was blind.

In town there are many lights. I go to one that's foxred. Inside, there are many women with hair cut like bluff's edge. And some pale ones with rabbity teeth. They are drinking that belly-low-water, trying to get as slinky and sly as me. When I flash my long eyes, they remember the feathers at their throats and their small birdlike bones. We reach an understanding.

First Fox understood that kits were in her belly. She licked herself. Inside, they felt her rough tongue teach spoor and hawthorn tunnel. Learned wrapback trails and logloops. Heard foxwords clicking on her tongue and teeth. Felt the sun padding its path across her belly.

There are men here, too. There are the evasive eyes of gray-suited men who think they're wolves. There are hands that snap-trap the flesh in dark corners. There are the growly words that smell like old meat on the teeth of urging men. But I got savvy. I know some tricks of my own! I take the smoky light into my nails and scratch my sign on their groins. Now there's some action!

First Fox felt the tiny eyes seamed shut in her belly. She sang the moon free from its oak snag. She dug a den and lined it with twelve kinds of fur—her warrior's booty.

After the bartender quieted things down, swept up the broken glass, and gave *those mice, those hairless voles* some bitter-gut water, things were dull. So I sashayed out and nosed on down the road.

First Fox nudged her newborn kits. Two vixens in her image and three males the blue-gray of WaterFox. The sun tripled itself into riddles; the moon was dappled, whole, torn, and mute: such were the passings of the weeks. The kits learned to hunt on their own.

Now this place is full of ferns hanging down and men propped up on their elbows, talking about numbers and scores and other data-based gossip. I feel like the inside of an ant hill; pacing and tossing my hair this way and that. Just about when I'm wishing I had some spiky red heels and a skirt as high as my hopes, they turn from watching that face-box and snuffle back into their drinks. Except this one, who is looking the way I look when the mouse has cheated my hunger.

The Sun blew across the sky like a tumbleweed. The kits did not return. First Fox scented their path. She found them in the bloodsmell of leaves and dirt. Pieces of their fur stuck to a man-thing that had teeth like a nightmare. Her own teeth gnashed the emptiness. Back in her den, she dreamt the Hunting Dream, the one that has become our destiny.

Yeah, this one is lean and feral. His gray eyes have inherited the mists. So I know he has foxblood from way back in his clan.

The Dream came from the Far-a-Field: Find the man who took your kits and from him get more kits. So she tracked him to his wood-split den and said the word into the dew. She rose up from the grass, sleek and cheeky. Vixen-wise.

My feet start the prowl, long wide circles of indifferent passion. Past the rows of bent-backed men. My eyes glance sideways more interested in the grace of my strut. He sidles past the seated women with their tiny city-bitch eyes. My haunches quiver.

The man saw the red-black hair of the woman and her swaying walk.

I look directly into his face.

The man sees her wide eyes and is trapped. He reaches out . . .

. . . we touch.

Hansel, Gretel, and Ruby Redlips

The moon's a path
into the forest.
Gretel is thin
as rain.

Hansel
is resourceful:
his pockets
are heavy
with white
pebbles.
They look
like little skulls
in the moonlight.
He marks the way
shadows trap eyes.

Then the clouds
drift out
of the hollows
of trees
and cover
the moon.
Only the witch
can see
that darkness
is a piece of flint.

She is called Ruby Redlips,
the Bewitcher,
the stepmother's rival.

Her beauty is the mask
of hunger.
Her hunger is a frame
of bones.
So she has a pretty house,
when all others are splinters
and harsh words.
And if she knows
a few spells
to make her body softer,
who could it hurt
to use that wisdom?
Not Gretel
who needs to learn
a few tricks of her own,
and not Hansel
who is just young enough
to see Ruby
with refreshing innocence.
A resourceful boy
is a resourceful man
and with his blue eyes...!
Gretel only needs rouge
and a wink or two
but Ruby needs
the magic mirror
of a young man's love.

If you've heard
a different version
of this tale,
then maybe
you've talked to the wrong person:
like the stepmother
who was stuck
with the woodcutter
who gets drunk
every Friday night
in fits of remorse
for the loss
of his golden-haired children
and the kisses
of Ruby Redlips.

In the Haunted House

you must not be afraid
of the other face
in the mirror

you must learn to like
the sound of the third foot
following behind you

you must never forget
there's a black black door
that's been painted over
   papered over
   paneled over
which opens
every night
into your dreams

you must learn to love
the black candles
that light themselves
when the moon
is howling

One Thing, Too Much

We all love one thing too much.
Chocolate. Coffee. Liquor.

We all love one man too much.
He is too close.
Or too far away.
Or we haven't been introduced yet.

We all fear one thing too much.
Being alone. Dying.
The stranger at the door.

We all lose one thing too much.
Our hopes, the long needles
of desire, the resilient cheek.

We all *think* we know too much:
our neighbor's business,
our children's secrets,
how a rose unfolds from memory.

But we don't know
what our own backs
look like
unless we're willing to see
from a different perspective.
We don't know that the stranger
is the lover we've always waited for.

We don't know that death
is the way
we shake hands
with life.

We don't know that too much
of one thing
is like a burning woman
calling for more wood.

Cow

From a newspaper article: Tests show that
high-powered electrical fields might cause
biological changes in some animals.

I can see beyond my nose;
a strange tension is in the grass,
like a snake with wings.
I hear power humming in the roots.
My humid breath stirs up stony clouds.
I am no longer content
with my heavy hump-self.

Once the hills were horns of grass,
the sun a fly in prairie waters.
Once my tail swatted bugs and stars alike.

Now I am not so certain of trails
that follow fences, of herds
that change direction at the smell of storm
or water.

I'd rather follow the edge of cliffs,
and wonder what comes after.
Does thunder become salt
in its abyss, or bones the wind
stacks into the shape of sky?

They say I'm unnatural.
Dangerous. Like a scar
that grows its own body.

But yesterday a red calf
was born into the herd.
He had the face of a human
and his hooves were deformed, too.

Return of the Wolves

All through the valley, the people are whispering:
the wolves are returning, returning
to the narrow edge of our fields, our dreams.
They are returning the cold to us.
They are wearing the crowns of ambush,
offering the rank and beautiful snow-shapes
of dead sheep, an old man too deep in his cups,
the trapper's gnawed hands, the hunter's tongue.
They are returning the whispers of our lovers,
whose promises are less enduring than the wolves'.

Their teeth are carving the sky into delicate antlers,
carving dark totems full of moose dreams: meadows
where light grows with the marshgrass and water
is a dark wolf under the hoof.
Their teeth are carving our children's names
on every trail, carving night into a different bone—
one that seems to be part of my body's long memory.

Their fur is gathering shadows, gathering
the thick-teethed white-boned howl of their tribe,
gathering the broken-deer smell of wind
into their longhouse of pine and denned earth,
gathering me also, from my farmhouse
with its golden light and empty rooms, to the cedar
(that also howls its woody name to the cave of stars),
where I am silent as a bow unstrung
and my scars are not from loving wolves.

The Language of Fossils

(Vantage, Washington)

this desert is a plateau of light

small diggers live in the soft stone
tongues of ancient beasts

calcified waves *stillflow* under
the sulfur-bellied marmots
and badgers claw at the salty star-
fish that tremble into dust

these stone logs are only weathering
time, friend, waiting
for the Cascades to become ash
and the ocean's green winds
to transform the sky
into acres of ferns

what will we become?
cool shadows in the red
mineral belly of the earth?

fossils speak the language of *Ginkgo:*
vowels like flat stones
with the carbonized wings
of leaf and beetle
and consonants like a bone
caught in the earth's throat

diceratheriym:
rhino pillowed in lava
layers of basalt bone
calcite   dolomite   pyrite
stratas of chalky diatoms
agate   flint   chert

what language is my passing
shadow? my name is lost
off the Columbia's cliffs:
immersed in silica and water
it will become an opal
with a woman's soul

An arrowhead whispers *flight!*
All the dark birds,
but one,
rush from the river
leaving only the stillness
of their language.

Star Light

Why aren't the heavens bright
with accumulated star light?

We are the visitors into
the dry interior.
This is fossil country
with names like major points
of interest: Wasteway,
Reservoir, Hartline.

Near Creston, we spot
two short-eared owls flying
over the constellations of sage.

The light that drifts
so slowly down
upon the Buttes
is a question
of years. We all travel
at a finite speed: the light,
the gift of muscle and bone.

What we owe to the light
—from stars blind
in their empty sockets—
is not lost in the retinas
of our souls.
Handspans of papyrus
to laser: all the star light

is a visible sphere
at the base of the brain.
Here is the song of the infinite.

Nightly, coyote songs ascend
into the sky
where calcified stars still shine
their shell-like light upon us.
We absorb it, becoming more
like dawn.

Birdwatching at Fan Lake

Our blue boat drifts
on the flat-shelled water.

In my lap: the red Book of Birds,
genesis of egg and feather

in the leavened air, begetting
the moist nests of osprey

and the mallard that floats
like bread on the water.

Around the lake are dark crowns
of granite and tall reeds with eyes

that burn gold in afternoon sun.
We eat salt crackers, green apples,

round cheese. On the shore,
a woman bends for a bright towel,

a white horse chews on wood.
The creek sings: *dribblestone,*

pebblelarvae. The red faces
of salamanders are wise

under the green bracken.
Waxwings sing to a chokecherry sun,

their throats shrill glass whistles.
We check our lists, compare.

Mine has notes like: the birds fly
into the white corridor of the sky.

Or: does the ruffed grouse's drumming
enter into the memories of trees?

Lately, we've talked less, been less
sure of each other. Love, why

travel this far to find rarity
and remain silent

in the curved wing of our boat?
Your hand on the oar is enough

for me to think of love's migration
from the intemperate heart to halcyon soul.

You point to a kingfisher,
whose eggs are laid on fish bones.

The fish are fin to the fisher's crest.
On a rocky beach, a killdeer keens,

orange-vested children pull up canoes,
camp smoke nests on the leafy water.

You take my hand and call it *wing*.
Sunlight is reborn in the heart

of the wild iris. Its purple shadows
sway over the root-dark fish.

Look: the long-necked herons
in the green-billed water

are pewter. Their wet-ash wings wear
medallions of patience. We drift on,

buoyed by the tiny currents between us,
the light long-legged, the wind

full of hearts that beat quick
and strong.

Burning the Fields

Rubbing his face with a red bandana,
the farmer burns his fields.
Somewhere, the red-tailed hawk
is awkwardless in the smoking air.

My shadow belongs to *smoke:*
the farmer is lost in its haze.
Grass curls in the cantering flames.

At the edge of steaming fields,
the wild grass keeps no promises,
empty of footprints, full
of skeletons puzzling the roots.

We all hope for a darkness
we can see. Somewhere, a nighthawk
dreams of the lean wind's promise.

Coyote Council

We gather on the Bluff.
The Wise Old Ones portend our future
in entrails. They say the air smells
of blood: the wind is blowing from the city.
They say our cunning is a true voice,
our dance against bullets a high power.
We are learning why we have waited.
The reason for hunger is remembered:
our ribs are the harps of the desert.
The reason for running is remembered:
our teeth shred the wind.
The reason for crying at the moon
is remembered: our breath is burning up
the last of the human nights.

Helix Aspersa

The typical garden snail breathes
and excretes through the same orifice,
reducing the loss
of moisture which has sifted through
the nets of conifer needles, diminished
to mist by the time it clings to the green collar
of trillium leaves. The snail is without
false expectations: whatever's left over
is life.

I am not dissatisfied with things as they are
but I wonder if it thinks the moon is a spindle-shaped shell,
smearing a glistening trail of stars?
And does it consciously fear thorns, droughts,
the windless volcanic ash? Or does it believe
the whole world is underneath, where the porous air
is full of fluid circles,
and weathering is a natural mercy?
No, it has no insight; it's as common as clover.
Observe its two front tentacles
which scent leaf-mold and lance leaf.
Its two longer tentacles are feeble eyes,
sensing only the light
which fogs its lusterless shell,
and the shadows that are boneless and flourishing.

I'm not without compassion
but I can't accept this inability to dream
beyond one's self. Yet the snail has a special knowledge:
creeping twenty-three inches an hour
it shifts its perceptions slowly.
Does it bore even itself?
Or is it enough that its evolutionary patience
has awarded it with practical intelligence:
it seeks decay on its own level.
And, finally, here is a curious fact:
although it travels great distances,
over liverwort, slime streams, and stone,
it tends to return to its point of origin,
where it contours its body-foot
to the fertile soil and observes life
revolving around it in concentric seasons
of earthly abandonment
and need.

Calypso

(an endangered woodland orchid)

As we search for rare orchids in the spring rain,
>let us light the candles of moonlight.
>In our fingernails and face
>the icons of wind and leaf.

We'll know the Calypso orchid instantly: the full-
>magdalen lips, the magenta veil,
>the absence of stones in nearby soil.
>Endangered. Elusive. Female.

Under the burnt wick stems of buckthorn, a friar gray
>wren scratches the bell-shaped pile
>of leaves. Fiddlehead ferns tune
>the misty air.

On the moist paths we make deep in the moss, there
>are trilliums white-faced and holy.
>Mute, they listen for the finger-
>prints of wind.

Other trilliums, maroon, carrion-colored, wanton,
>their faces turning to earth, confess
>our secrets to the emissaries of flies.
>There in the candelabra of clouds,
>our prayers burn the ozone: make me rich,
>make me pretty, make me powerful, make
>me innocent.

We hope for a crown of pure air. We wait for an angel
      robed in green ferns. At our feet, the
      aluminum cans of poachers dazzle slugs.
      Chainsaw oil is the myrrh of moss.

If we are made in God's image, let us imagine that our skin
      is the plateau of Her breath,
      our eyes the inner maps of stars,
      and our tongues the tongues of orchids,
      our only testament the chime of rain on wings.

Not the polysyllables of toxins and polluted aquifers,
      our bones just commas in cancerous flesh,
      our skin a controversy of yellow rain
      and bee shit, our blood an alphabet of pesticides,
      our fingers like combs untangling the gray air,
      our voices crying: Bless *me,* Bless *me.*

Avocados, on a Tree

These thin green girls
with the still-babies
in their bellies
dance in the wind,
their pitted faces peering
from behind dark leaves.

They are tiny goddesses
lighting green candles
in the night.
They are the whores
who remain innocent, green, unripe,
'though their legs are streaked
with semen.

They are windy voices
caught in the pear-shaped capes
of mourning.

They are the green flames
vegetarians dine by.
They are the leaf-ribbed ghosts
of abandoned daughters,
the ocean's rain.

They are green emeralds,
fists of rebellion.

They are the fruit
on the wooden plate
which you give to me.
They are the folded hands in my lap,
the peelings spiraling
like gift ribbon.

In death, they hang on,
withered black umbrellas—
while our blood quickens
with the abundance
of our fruitful flesh.

They are the wrinkled-winged bats,
eyeing the day
without direction.
They are our old faces
prepared to fall
back into the earth.

They are drums of silence,
rhythms in a vegetal tongue.

They are the green spoons
we use to pour water with,
to wash our thighs
after making love.

They are the vials of perfume
the tropic night breaks.

They are the raw wine,
the lies lovers still believe in,
even while knowing the fruit falls not
far from the tree.

They are the bell-toned singers:
whole nights are forgiven
in their green throats.

If You Hold a Blue Rock

If you hold a blue rock to your ear,
you will hear the ancient river
that kept it as its heart,
the dry wind that used it for its tongue,
and the earth that promised it a mouth of fire.

A speckled rock is from the dream
of a galloping appaloosa.
The herd sings its Ceremony of Grass
and their dream-stones fly from their hooves
into the spattered sky.

A black rock has the bear's soul caught
in his last sleep. His song circles
the stone, giving it the illusion
of fur.

All yellow rocks keep the secrets of Owls.
All green rocks are the breaths of plants
singing in nightly joy.

A red fist-sized rock is the love
of a man and a woman as their bodies sing
on the grass.

A gray stone is naturally mournful.
It is a word from the common language of the dead.
Keep it. Someday you will understand.

Solstice Moon Chant

(sixty-four ways of looking at the moon)

natal moon
stony crone
salt apple
oaten eye
sky cataract
silken coin
one-eyed cat
milky cup
ivory onion
sand dollar
squat olmec
snake skin
oriental oracle
ice star coral
albino coal
dino eye
blow fish
blood bubble
wind rind
fairy ring
cowry finger
whiskey horse
squash blossom
barley bird
corn maiden

babylonian bell
chalk baby
skull caulking
stalking hound
death's head
medicine wheel
winter mask
lily ash
camas belly
salmon opal
white orchid
moon canoe
water diamond
plain pulp
conch shell
ram horn
sulfur vulture
silver conch
poison cup
ankle bell
arctic arroyo
sky door
white kohl
frost fan
sky rip

bone basket
melted heart
wax marble
drum skin
ancient amah
brittle cradle
crazy karma

pale palm
glass melon
woolen wind
dusky medallion
pretty woman
holy woman
ah! omen!

The Green of the Oceans

1

the green of the oceans of winds is surely a mistranslation
of god, although I prefer little black Isis, who is sister
to Nut and her hump-backed extensions of sky.
    Or are we imprinted
by the blood-red hooves of the Horse Goddess? And so we dream
of the houris, those dark long-eyed women dancing in paisley saris.

2

yes, the oceans of green transform us, bringing us closer
to dawn, the dolphin's secret smile. And so, the oracle is lost
like a bone from the tongue. The moon goddess cast the runic air:
what agrees with the bear-shirted warrior
    does not agree with the soul.
Berserker, aquavit spearholder! Watch the Baltic milky green stars
pulse and sink hissing into the sea. Or put it this way: the fiery
green oceanic winds are why each of us is a little bit sacred.

3

Most people's god must be worn on a chain around the neck,
especially in the fields of night. But I'm as pagan
as a straw goddess tossed on the green wind. Give me your hand
which is rough against my breast and attendant
to my breathing. My breast is a rounded thing, unlike the ocean,
although the swell of salt on your lips is deep.
The wind holds its shamanistic voice until the night has turned
its dark lavender body toward the earth.
Then whatever is left after our loving glows around us like god,
a single syllable, and as fine as the threads of diamonds.

There are no horses in this poem, Bo

1

The only wild thing
is the moon.
A woman offers it
a spur of sugar.

2

In my dreams, I'm that woman.
And the moon grazes at meadow's edge.

3

Hat pulled low,
a man rides
a white-maned moon
out of town
at sunrise.
From my window above
the Silver Crescent Saloon,
I lean out,
a tarnished coin
in my palm.

4

The one-moon town still exists:
a false front defining the horizon.

5

In these western hills
there are pockets of wild moons.
Rugged-ribbed, shaggy-eyed moons:
unlike our domestic kind
which we've trained to be calm
reflections in our water troughs.

6

Environmentalists say wild moons bite
too close to the earth.
The land is eroded:
the rain rides its own
Chiseling Trail.

7

We call those wild ones *lunas,*
which is Spanish for moon
and American for crazy.
It's a respectable name
in the western tradition.
A Sioux leader was called
Crazy Moon.
Shoot-outs were staged at High Moon.
Rustlers rode black moons;
posses rode theirs into the dust.

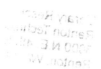

8

Where I live
moons race rivers
and win.
Moons sometime canter
into lakes
and are never seen again.

9

The unknown is a dark moon.
The unexpected is a moon of a different color.

10

Moons are given to brides
on their wedding nights.
Children rock on moons.
Teenagers moon around
on street corners.
Moons are part of divorce settlements.

11

Some moons are stuffed
when they die.
But most moons are put out
to pasture.

12

If I promised you a string of moons
(roan-colored moons,
star-blaze moons,

buckskin moons,
spotted moons),
would you come back
and race the stars with me?

13

Ah. I don't have any moons,
remember?
My sweet offer remains
in my out-stretched hand.
But
if I had a bridle
of fine Mexican silver,
I'd give it to you.

If I had reins that jingled,
I'd give them to you.

If I had a blanket
the seven colors of a Taos sun,
I'd give it to you.

It may seem I'm giving you
only what I don't have
or have need of,
but wait:
it's only my shy way
of asking you
for the moon.

Jacques: For a gift of wood

(Grenoble, 1989)

1

in the next room you sleep
with small Isabelle
who is a tree
of midnight blue

2

eight trees open up
in your hands
eight limbs of man and woman
with the great root
between you

3

Isabelle lives alone
with a cat named Moses
who was born in the rain

she gathers the animals within:
the charcoal monkeys as they grin in horror
from the papery dreams
of the Turkish artist,
and tiny creatures whose hands disappear
in the darkness

4

Isabelle has the gift
of loving many, the way sky

loves the light
in the center of trees

5

so, perhaps there is nothing
between you but the luminous sleep
of innocent apple blossoms

6

in your house
the female shapes
of honey-colored wood
find their secret way
to your hands

7

Noyer, orme
you give me a curl of names
poirier
in the mysterious language of the seventh tree
cerisier

Isabelle is the tree that will not marry
frêne
she's not the bridal blossoms
drifting, weightless as the moon's
own blossoming
mélèze, chêne

she's with you as you dream,
serene, la belle dame, untamed.

The Migration of Trees

Wood on a journey as intimate
as a door, a bed, a crutch:

Open the door. Inside: a room
with a clock that ticks
like the tramp of boots.
A window shaped like a bandage,
the cut still oozing.
A table: its heart still beating
the circular weathering.
And on the table, a stack of letters:
pale shavings we mark
with the ax strokes
of our desires and regrets.

This is the bed, covered
with white sheets so that the tree
can dream of snow.
And the woman who lies down there
can sleep her whole life
away
dreaming of strong limbs.

When she is old
and her legs go slowly
into the migration,
she can look at the sky
as if it were a hill

and all the trees green crutches
to grasp on to, their voices
as quiet as sawdust,
their leaves falling like birthmarks
onto the earth, her weariness.

Duck Hunting

when the birds detach themselves
from our sights,
falling clumsily into their own shadows,
have they changed our relationship
with the sky?

their eyes film over,
like the dusty holes between two mountains
and the sudden drop of sky

it is men who want what they cannot reach
without bringing it down
to their level

in the early dawn,
their cigarettes glow like little eyes

and then, above, a dark bird
no bigger than a young girl's heart.

Dream Without a City

the animals paint on cave walls
birds create aerial bridges

trees root music out of the earth
insects worship on altars of air

water weaves wide shawls in the valleys
everywhere the people are happy

everywhere their hands hold their lovers' faces
the animals sing to be fruitful

the birds teach returnings
the trees stand for commitment

and the water
the water

it breaks out of the womb
and opens its eyes

About the Author

It is rare for a poet to also excel as a visual artist, but Anita Endrezze beautifully bridges the two worlds of the visual arts and the literary arts. Her poems have appeared in numerous magazines, including *National Geographic* and *Yellow Silk,* and in several anthologies, including *Dancing on the Rim of the World* (University of Arizona, 1990). Her paintings have been widely shown, and they have appeared on book covers in the U.S. and in Europe.

Endrezze also bridges two cultures: Native American and European. She is of half-Yaqui and half-European heritage. She is professional storyteller as well as a poet, fiction writer, translator, and artist. She has taught classes for elementary, high school, university, and community college students, as well as for various community groups, and she has presented her work in France and Denmark.

She received her B.A. in teaching and M.A. in creative writing at Eastern Washington University. She currently lives in Spokane, Washington, with her husband and two children.

Acknowledgments

Thanks to the publishers of the following books and journals, where some of the poems in this collection appeared in these or earlier versions. Poems are reprinted here by permission of the author.

Anthology of Twentieth Century Native American Poetry, Harper and Row, 1988: "Birdwatching at Fan Lake," "The Girl Who Loved the Sky," "Hansel, Gretel, and Ruby Redlips," "The Language of Fossils," "Return of the Wolves," "Reviewing Past Lives While Leaf-Burning," "Song Maker," "Star Light"

A Nation Within, Pacific Quarterly Moana, Vol. 8, No. 1, 1983: "Helix Aspersa"

Archae, Spring 1991, Fascicle 1: "In the Horizontal Sky"

Auch das Gras Hat Ein Lied, Herder and Company, 1988: "If You Hold a Blue Rock," "Song Maker"

The Berkeley Poetry Review, No. 25, 1991–1992: "Mistranslations, or The Green of the Oceans," "There are no horses in this poem, Bo," "Waking"

Burning the Fields, Confluence Press, 1983: "Burning the Fields," "Claiming Lives," "Helix Aspersa," "Last Harvest," "The Magician's Daughter," "November," "Sanctuary"

Carriers of the Dream Wheel, Harper and Row, 1975: "Canto Llano"

The Chariton Review, Vol. 9, No. 2, Fall 1983: "The Girl Who Loved the Sky," "Return of the Wolves"

Dancing on the Rim of the World, University of Arizona, 1990: "The Dieter's Daughter," "I was born," "The light that passes through stones," "The Mapmaker's Daughter"

Deep Down Things, Washington State University, 1990: "The Language of Fossils," "The Medicine Woman's Daughter," "One Thing Too Much," "Ways to See"

Ergo!, Bumbershoot Festival Commission, 1986: "Fox-Woman Goes Man-Hunting"

Hungry Poets Cookbook, Applezabba Press, 1987, "In the Kitchen"

The Kenyon Review, Vol. XIII, No. 4, Fall 1991: "Duck Hunting," "The Migration of Trees," "Perceptions of Three Birches"

l'arbre a paroles No. 65, Fall 1989: "If You Hold a Blue Rock," "Star Light"

National Geographic, Vol. 180, No. 4, October 1991: "Birdwatching at Fan Lake," "The Language of Fossils"

The North People, Blue Cloud Quarterly, 1983: "The Alchemist's Wife," "Cow," "Coyote Council," "Reviewing Past Lives While Leaf-Burning," "What We Believe"

Parole Nel Sangue, Mondadori, 1991: "Song Maker"

Poesie-Rencontres, No. 25, 1989: "Song Maker"

Poetes Indiens D'Amerique (Poesie Presente), No. 70/71, 1989: "Dream Without a City," "Duck Hunting," "If You Hold a Blue Rock," "In the Horizontal Sky," "The light that passes through stones," "The Migration of Trees," "Twelve Love Poems," "Ways to See"

Poetry East, No. 32, Fall 1991: "Cow," "In the House of Animals"

Poetry Northwest, Vol. XXIII, No. 4, 1982–1983: "Helix Aspersa," "Sanctuary"

Rain in the Forest, Light in the Trees, Owl Creek Press, 1983: "November"

Shaman's Drum, Spring 1988, No. 12: "Dream Without a City"

Songs from this earth on turtle's back, Greenfield Review, 1983: "If You Hold a Blue Rock," "Song Maker"

Southern Poetry Review, Fall 1983: "Reviewing Past Lives While Leaf-Burning"

The Spokesman-Review, April 22, 1990: "Duck Hunting," "Helix Aspersa"

Voice, Vol. 74, No. 16, 1990: "The Girl Who Loved the Sky," "What We Believe"

The Wire Harp, 1989: "Dream Without a City," "Duck Hunting," "The light that passes through stones," "Storm"

Wooster Review, No. 8, Spring 1988: "Calendars," "Jacques: For a gift of wood," "One Thing Too Much," "Searching for the One in My Dreams," "Storm," "There are no horses in this poem, Bo"

Words in the Blood, Meridian, 1984: "What We Believe"

Yellow Silk, No. 24, Autumn 1987: "I Give You," "The Jester's Daughter," "These Are Roses You've Never Given Me"

Yellow Silk, No. 25, Winter 1987: "Sunflower Woman"

Yellow Silk, No. 35, Winter 1990–1991: "The Mapmaker's Daughter"

Yellow Silk Anthology, Crown/Harmony Books, 1990: "I Give You"

Design by Ken Sánchez.

Text set in Bembo,
using the KI/Composer and Linotron 202N.
Typeset by Blue Fescue Typography and Design,
Seattle, Washington.

Printed on recycled, acid-free paper
by Maple-Vail, York, Pennsylvania.